HAUNTED

BATTLEFIELDS

VERDUN

HISTORY AND LEGEND
BY

EARLE RICE JR.

PURPLE TOAD
PUBLISHING

HAUNTED
BATTLEFIELDS

ANTIETAM by Russell Roberts
GETTYSBURG by Russell Roberts
LITTLE BIGHORN by Earle Rice Jr.
VERDUN by Earle Rice Jr.

PUBLISHER'S NOTE:
The data in this book has been researched in depth, and to the best of our knowledge is factual. Although every measure is taken to give an accurate account, Purple Toad Publishing makes no warranty of the accuracy of the information and is not liable for damages caused by inaccuracies.

ABOUT THE AUTHOR:
Earle Rice Jr. is a former senior design engineer and technical writer in the aerospace, electronic-defense, and nuclear industries. He has devoted full time to his writing since 1993 and is author of over 70 published books. Rice is listed in *Who's Who in America* and is a member of the Society of Children's Book Writers and Illustrators, the League of World War I Aviation Historians, the Air Force Association, and Disabled American Veterans.

Printing 1 2 3 4 5 6 7 8 9

Publisher's Cataloging-in-Publication Data
Rice Jr., Earle.
  Verdun / Earle Rice, Jr..
    p. cm.
Includes bibliographic references and index.
ISBN 9781624691164
1. Verdun, Battle of, Verdun, France, 1916. 2. World War, 1914-1918—France—Verdun.   I. Series: Haunted battlefields.
 D545
 940.4272

Library of Congress Control Number: 2014945189

ebook ISBN: 9781624691171

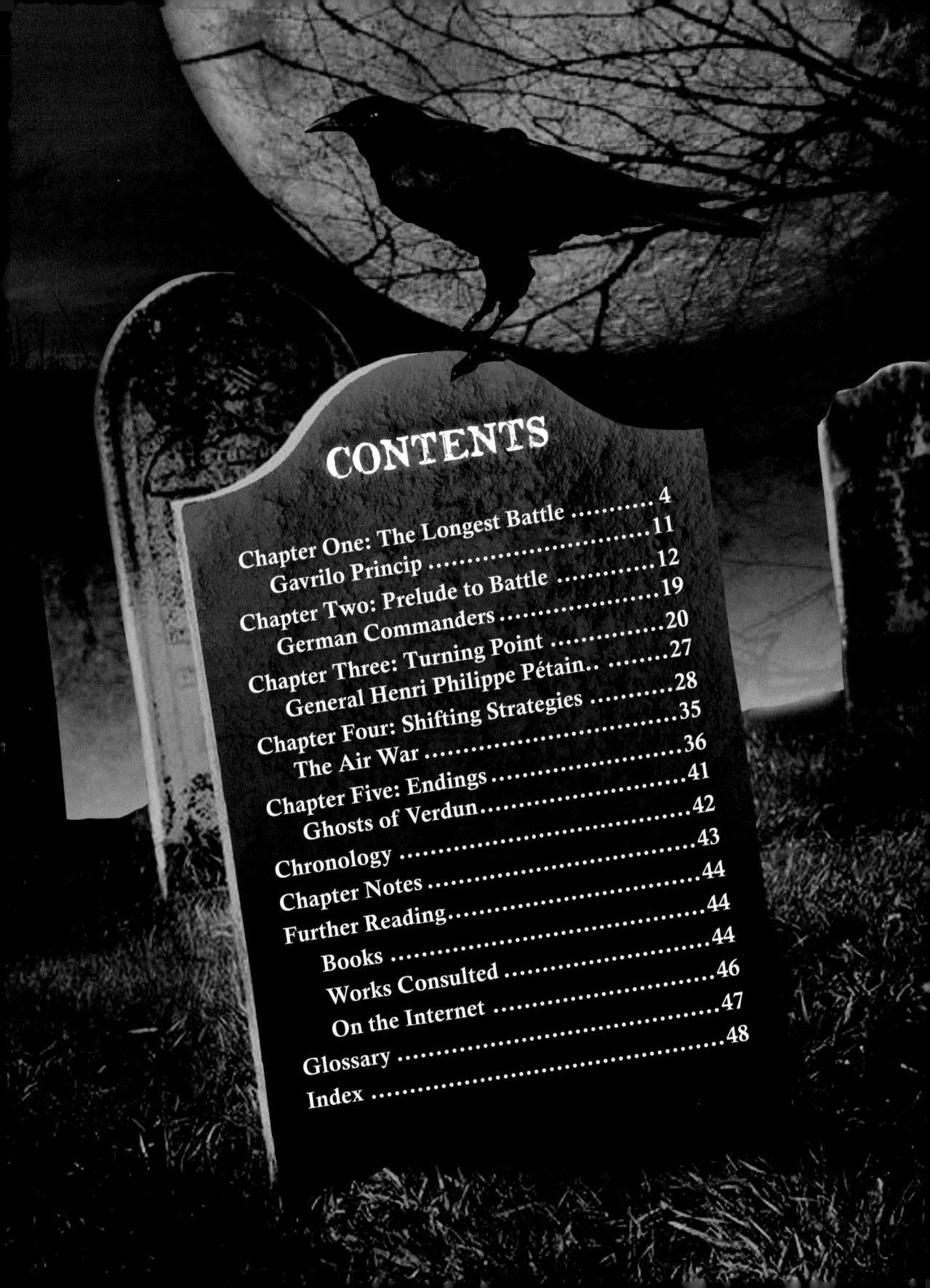

CONTENTS

CHAPTER

ONE

THE LONGEST BATTLE

The French named the hill *Le Mort Homme*—the Dead Man. Many years ago, long before World War I, the body of an unidentified man found on the hill had inspired the name. With the coming of the war—then known as the Great War—the name became infinitely more appropriate.

On March 6, 1916, the VI German Reserve Army Corps began its advance on Le Mort Homme during the Battle of Verdun. A heavy artillery bombardment preceded their attack. German soldiers thought that the rain of steel on the little hill would make it easy for them to overcome Mort Homme's French defenders. By the end of March, German casualties numbered 81,607, against French losses of 89,000. Mort Homme remained in French hands. The hill's name was taking on a larger meaning.

Augustin Cochin, an officer of the French 146th Regiment, spent April 9–14 in the Mort Homme trenches and did not see a single German soldier. He recalled "the last two days soaked in icy mud, under terrible bombardment, without any shelter other than the narrowness of the trench. . . . The Boche [Germans] did not attack,

★ ★ ★ ★ ★ ★ ★ ★ ★ ★ ★ ★ ★ ★ ★

German soldiers assault *Le Mort Homme*

French soldiers in a trench use a periscope to watch for enemy activity. Periscopes were used to monitor enemy movements without exposing the user to deadly shot and shell.

naturally, it would have been too stupid . . . result: I arrived there with 175 men, I returned with 34, several half mad . . . not replying any more when I spoke to them."[1]

Another French soldier on the way to Le Mort Homme, noted, "[M]y battalion comes straight from the land behind the front-lines, the men are exhausted and did not sleep. The battalion consists of 800 men—the battalion that we are here to replace lost 800 men."[2]

Conditions were hardly better for the attackers. A German soldier remembered, "One soldier was going insane with thirst and drank from a pond covered with a greenish layer near Le Mort-Homme. A corpse was afloat in it; his black countenance face down in the water and his abdomen swollen as if he had been filling himself up with water for days now."[3] Such were the horrors of Le Mort Homme in 1916.

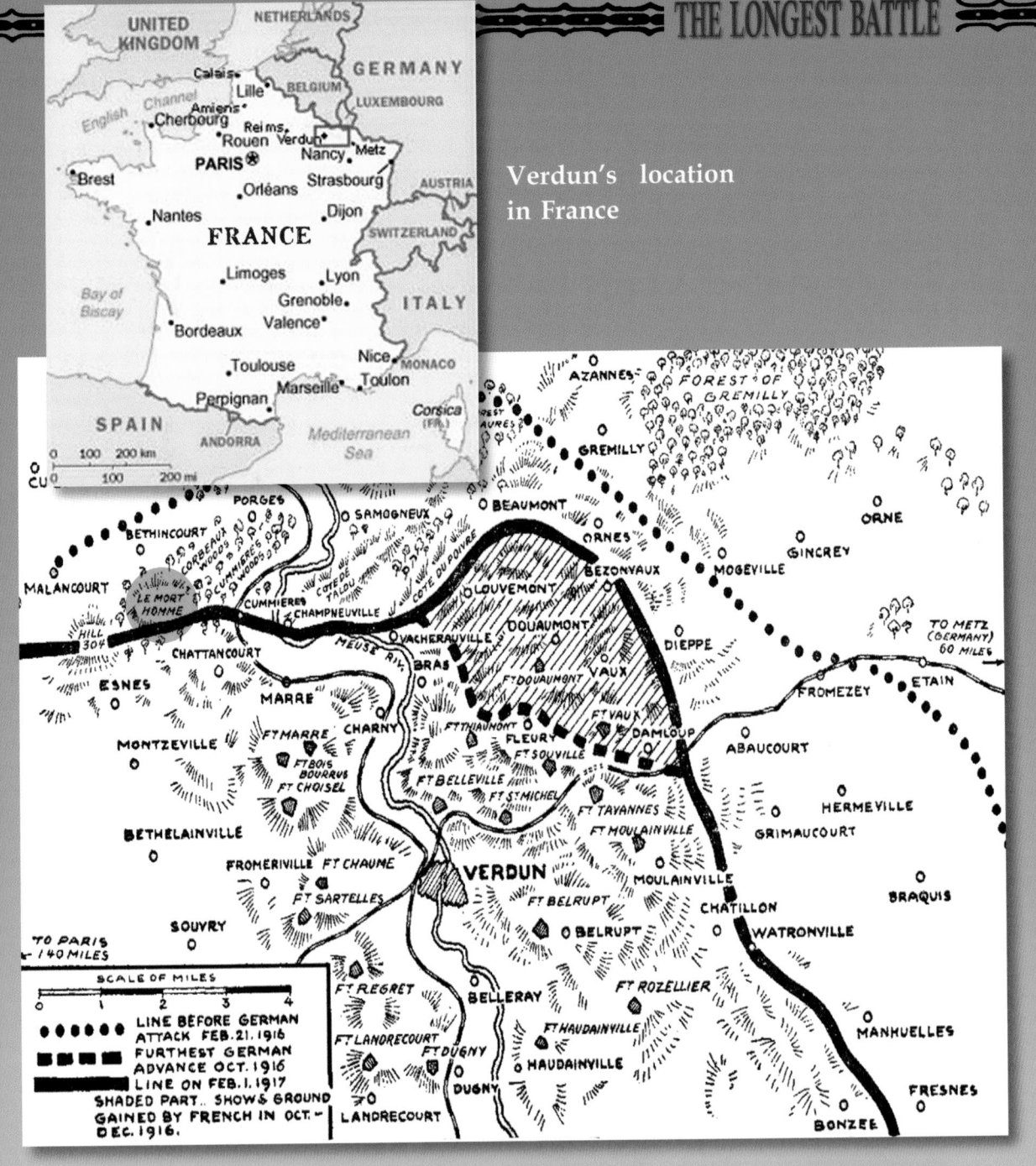

Verdun's location in France

Le Mort Homme, circled in red, was the scene of some of the fiercest fighting during the Battle of Verdun. After three months of fighting, the Germans seized the hill from the French in late May 1916, only to give it back to them in August.

Today, almost a century later, visitors to the Verdun battlefield often find ghostly evidence of the fighting long past, particularly in the vicinity of Le Mort Homme. Many visitors have looked up at the sound of an old aircraft to see a German fighter plane of World War I vintage, trailing smoke and flame across the sky, before disappearing behind the crest of Côte (hill) 304. Local folks do not admit to the existence of ghostly phenomena, but they believe the sightings are of Oswald Boelcke. Boelcke was a World War I German ace and aerial tactician who was shot down over Verdun.

Ghostly presences are common at battlefields and other scenes where death rules the day, and few battlefields surpass Verdun in numbers slain. German Fifth Army commander Crown Prince Wilhelm described the Verdun campaign as "the Mill on the Meuse, which ground to dust the hearts as well as the bodies of our men."[4] This "meat-grinder" of a battle began on February 21, 1916, and lasted until December 18, 1916. The Battle of Verdun was the longest battle of World War I. Its haunting memories linger with the French to this very day.

In 1914, Europe was a tinder box waiting to catch fire. The spark that set Europe aflame for the next four years was struck by Gavrilo Princip in Sarajevo on June 28. He was a Bosnian Serb who opposed the annexation of Bosnia and Herzegovina by the Habsburg throne of Austria-Hungary. When the Habsburg archduke and his wife visited Sarajevo on that day, Princip shot them both dead. And the winds of war blew across the armed camp of Europe.

Archduke Franz Ferdinand, his wife Sophie, Duchess of Hohenberg, with their three children.

Word spread across the globe about the Archduke's assassination. War was on the horizon.

Early in the twentieth century, Europe was split into two major coalitions: the Triple Alliance of Germany, Austria-Hungary, and Italy—the Central Powers; and the Triple Entente of France, Russia, and Great Britain—the Allies. In this alliance-dominated hotbed of imperial, territorial, and economic rivalries, war became predictable if not inevitable. Princip's assassination of the archduke provided a convenient excuse—if in fact one was needed—for the guns to speak in August 1914. In reality, conflicting international interests paved the road to World War I.

Austria-Hungary wanted to expand its boundaries to the Balkans. Germany sought to establish itself as the preeminent European power and challenge Great Britain's claim to naval superiority. France, historically, was threatened by Germany, particularly since its defeat in the Franco-Prussian War (1870–1871) and its resultant loss of most of the Alsace-Lorraine. Britain eyed Germany's growing naval might with alarm. And Russia, viewing itself as champion of the Slavs, hungered to expand into the Balkans and extend its borders to the sea.

On July 28, 1914, Austria-Hungary, after its demands for reparations were only partially met, declared war on Serbia. Within a week, every alliance-driven major power had entered "the war to end all wars" (as World War I was often called). Russia mobilized against Austria-Hungary, whereupon Germany declared war against Russia on August 1. Germany advanced into neutral Luxembourg and Belgium and declared war on France on August 3.

Great Britain's King George V appeals to Britons to come to the aid of their country in this famous recruiting poster. Crowds of Englishmen answer his call and flock to a recruitment center in 1914.

Great Britain reacted by declaring war on Germany on August 4 for invading neutral Belgium. Austria-Hungary declared war against Russia on August 6. Despite its obligations to the Triple Alliance, Italy remained neutral for a time. It claimed its responsibilities to the alliance were voided because Austria-Hungary had started the war. In truth, Italy hoped to wait until a winner became clear before casting its lot with either side. Across the Atlantic, the United States was torn by conflicting ethnic sympathies and became a temporary onlooker to history's first modern war.

Gavrilo Princip was a Bosnian nationalist. He was born into a Serb peasant family on July 25, 1894, in Obljaj, Bosnia. At age eighteen, he tried to enlist for military service with Bosnia during the First Balkan War, but was rejected as medically unfit. His rejection motivated him to do something exceptionally brave to prove himself to others.

Princip then received training in terrorist methods by the Serbian secret society known as the Black Hand, or Union of Death. He and five fellow activists conspired to assassinate a top Austro-Hungarian official or a member of the Habsburg ruling family. They figured such a vile and senseless act would lead to Slavic unity and independence. On May 26, 1914, the conspirators made their way from Belgrade to Sarajevo, the capital of Bosnia and Herzegovina.

On June 28, Archduke Franz Ferdinand, heir to the Austro-Hungarian empire, and his consort Sophie, duchess of Hohenberg, arrived in Sarajevo on an official visit. When his procession moved through town, one of the conspirators tossed a bomb at his car. It missed and exploded under the following car. Several bystanders were wounded. Four other conspirators lost their nerve and took no action.

Later, while on the way to the hospital, the archduke's car took a wrong turn and stopped in front of Princip to back up. Princip pulled his pistol, mounted the car's dashboard, and shot the archduke and duchess at point-blank range. Sophie died instantly; the archduke died within the hour. Austria-Hungary held Serbia responsible. Using the assassination as an excuse for war, Austria-Hungary set in motion a string of events leading to World War I.

Gavrilo Princip

CHAPTER

TWO

PRELUDE TO BATTLE

At the outset of World War I, the Germans slashed quickly through Belgium on the Western Front and advanced on Paris and the English Channel. They were led by General Helmuth J. L. von Moltke. Great Britain and France—the Allies—had expected the Germans to attack along the Franco-German frontier. When the Allies under French General Joseph J. C. Joffre finally recognized that the main German thrust was instead in the west, they met and stopped the German advance at the Marne. By autumn 1914, the two sides had established a continuous static front from the Belgian coast to Switzerland.

In this first modern war, the machine gun and artillery revolutionized combat tactics. The advantage shifted to the defense. A defender could bring up reserves to limit a penetration much faster than an attacker could advance his reserves and artillery to exploit a breakthrough. The Germans recognized the change in tactics far ahead of the Allies. They adopted a flexible defense system using two or more heavily fortified trench lines. If an attacker broke through the first line, he would face withering machine-gun and artillery fire from second- or third-line defenses.

★ ★ ★ ★ ★ ★ ★ ★ ★ ★ ★ ★ ★ ★ ★ ★ ★

The German 08 model of the Maxim system machine gun, was the basic German machine gun of World War I. This gun is said to have killed more people than any other weapon of war.

Both sides suffered appalling losses in 1915. French casualties totaled 1,292,000 and British losses numbered 279,000, against some 612,000 killed, wounded, and missing Germans. Heavy fighting scarred the land from the North Sea to the Swiss Alps, but the opposing battle lines remained virtually unchanged by year's end.

In 1916, both sides planned great offensives to break the stalemate on the Western Front. The Germans, now under General Erich von Falkenhayn, struck first.

Falkenhayn's strategy viewed England as the Great Adversary of the Central Powers. If France could be defeated first, he reasoned, the "breaking point would be reached and England's best sword knocked out of her hand."[1] Operationally, his analysis translated into a need for a limited offensive at a vital point that would "compel the French to throw in every man they have. If they do so the forces of France will bleed to death."[2] And the Triple Entente alliance would collapse.

Falkenhayn was chief of the German general staff. He well knew that his forces could not remain on the defensive. The

General Erich von Falkenhayn attempted to destroy the French Army in a battle of attrition at Verdun. The French were bled white in the ten-month battle, but the Germans suffered almost as many casualties.

The crush of German high-explosives turned the battlefield in the Verdun sector into a virtual moonscape in 1916. A century later, unexploded shells are still being uncovered in the lush, green rolling hills.

Allies had greater resources in men and matériel (military materials and equipment). Moreover, their numbers were increasing faster than those of the Central Powers. Falkenhayn had to act decisively and soon. With Russia all but defeated in the east, he selected Verdun as his target on the Western Front.

In Roman times, before Gaul became France, Verdun had been a fortress. It had been rebuilt many times by Vauban, the great French military engineer, Napoleon III, and others, and was strengthened by concrete and armor. After German heavy artillery shattered similar forts at Liège and Namur in Belgium in 1914, the French lost confidence in all their fortifications. They stripped Verdun's fortress guns and sent them off for use in the field. The French also reduced their number of garrison forces. Even so, as Falkenhayn correctly calculated, the French would never give up Verdun—whatever the cost of its defense. It was a matter of national pride.

Fort Douaumont was the largest and highest fort in a ring of nineteen major defensive forts protecting the city of Verdun. Surprisingly, it was entered and occupied without a fight by a small German raiding party.

In 1916, Verdun stood in the middle of a narrow salient that jutted into German-controlled territory. It lay 160 miles due east of Paris, split in two by the River Meuse. A ring of 19 major and 40 minor forts, with 75- and 155-millimeter (mm) cannon and machine guns, surrounded the town. Fort Douaumont (pronounced DOO-oh-mon) was the mightiest of these. It stood closest to the front lines. The reduced garrison of the Verdun region numbered about 65,000 soldiers.

A small narrow-gauge railway supplied Verdun with some food and matériel, but it was inadequate for the bulk of French munitions, rations, and personnel. Because of Verdun's remote location, it depended on the departmental road from

Bar-le-Duc for most of its provisions. By contrast, the Germans were well-supplied by recently built roads and light railways connecting to their nearby base at Metz.

In February 1916, the *Fortifiée de Verdun* (Fortified Region of Verdun or RFV) consisted of four regular and three reserve divisions under General Frédéric-Georges Herr. Facing them stood Crown Prince Wilhelm's Fifth Army, reinforced by ten divisions and a massive concentration of artillery—140,000 men for the attack and 2.7 million artillery shells. Along a French defensive front of eight miles, Falkenhayn had amassed one German division and 150 guns to each mile.

Falkenhayn designated his assault Operation *Gericht* (Judgment). His attack was to be preceded by a deluge of preparatory fire so that "no line is to remain unbombarded, no possibilities of supply unmolested, nowhere should the enemy feel himself safe."[3] He expected that the massive artillery barrage would reduce any French defenders to atoms.

Operation *Gericht* was scheduled to begin on February 12, 1916, but bad weather postponed its start from day to day. Snow and freezing rain persisted the following week. Poor visibility grounded observation balloons and aerial observers. Artillery spotters were blinded by the swirling snow. And the wait went on. The rains stopped on February 19, and a warming sun rose over the Meuse the next day. Operation *Gericht* was now set to begin before daybreak on February 21.

Crown Prince Wilhelm encouraged his troops with a stirring message: "The iron will of

Crown Prince Wilhelm, later known as Kaiser Wilhelm II

the sons of Germany is still unbroken and the German Army, when it moves to attack, stops for no obstacle."[4]

Across the Meuse, General Herr, commander of the RFV, issued a similarly rousing statement to Verdun's defenders: "Resist whatever the cost; let yourselves be cut to pieces on the spot rather than fall back."[5] Falkenhayn's campaign of attrition to "bleed France white"[6] was at last ready to launch.

French soldiers ride across a river on the way to Verdun.

General Erich von Falkenhayn was born into an old military family at Burg Bechau, West Prussia, in 1861. After graduating from cadet school, he joined the infantry and served as a military instructor in China. He was a member of the German staff during the Boxer Rebellion in 1900. After General Helmuth von Moltke's defeat in the Battle of the Marne, Falkenhayn replaced him as chief of the German general staff.

Though a brilliant staff officer, Falkenhayn lacked the determination and strategic grasp required for high command. His campaign of attrition at Verdun inflicted heavy casualties against the French, but the Germans suffered almost as many. He was relieved of command and sent to the Eastern Front in August 1916. After the war, Falkenhayn retired to his castle at Lindstadt, where he died, in the words of Alistair Horne, "plagued by bad dreams"[7] in 1922.

Crown Prince Wilhelm, the eldest son of Kaiser Wilhelm II, was an unusual kind of officer. Born in Potsdam in 1882, he was made a corporal at the age of seven. Slender of frame, he was a man of contrasts. Wilhelm loved opera and played the violin well. He enjoyed the life of a playboy prince and also aspired to military glory.

Though initially an amateur on the battlefield, Wilhelm developed into a first-rate strategist. Because of the bloodshed at Verdun, critics nicknamed him "the laughing murderer of Verdun."[8] A sensitive man, he was deeply affected by the label. He went on to achieve the status of an army group commander in the last two years of the war. Wilhelm died in 1951.

Crown Prince Wilhem (seated) with his officers, including General Eric von Falkenhayn standing behind, fourth from left.

CHAPTER

THREE

TURNING POINT

The soul-shattering thunder of the German guns spoke at 4:00 AM on February 21, 1916. Three 15-inch (380-millimeter) naval guns opened the barrage. The first shells targeted the bridges over the Meuse, the Bishop's Palace at Verdun, and the city's railway station. As the night sky gave way to morning's light, some 1,200 guns added their voices to the chorus of destruction at 7:00 am. The sound of their thunder was heard 150 miles (241 kilometers) away.

Mixed fire of shrapnel, high explosives, and poison gas was designed "to create a zone of death . . . where no Frenchman drew breath."[1] Shells shrieked down at a rate of 100,000 rounds per hour. Some two million shells struck the narrow triangle defined by Brabant, Ornes, and Verdun. Eighty thousand shells fell on the Caures Wood (*Bois des Caures*) alone, an area measuring only 1,422 x 875 yards (1,318 x 800 meters) in area.

A nine-hour torrent of steel and high explosives pummeled ravines, forests, trenches, and redoubts (strong points) and churned them into earthbound moonscapes. French defenders, hunkered down in trenches, shell holes, dug-outs, or other protective

★ ★ ★ ★ ★ ★ ★ ★ ★ ★ ★ ★ ★ ★ ★ ★

Wooded areas offered no protection to
the soldiers about to be caught in the
German barrage.

Soldiers were cut down left and right by wave after wave of bullets and artillery fire.

depressions, clutched the earth and waited, all helpless to control their fate in the face of imminent death. One French soldier later recalled the horror of clinging to life at Verdun: "The night is disturbed by light as clear as if it were day. The earth moves and shakes like jelly. And the men . . . at the frontline cannot hear anything but the drumfire, the moaning of wounded friends, the screams of hurt horses, the wild pounding of their own hearts, hour after hour, day after day, night after night."[2]

Falkenhayn's plan called for two days of full-scale bombardment, followed each day by the assault of the Crown Prince's shock divisions. At 4:00 PM on the first day, the murderous barrage lifted. German soldiers emerged from their *Stollen*—underground galleries, hastily burrowed out all along the attack zone— and advanced slowly across the pulverized wasteland. They moved not in a wave but in small groups, dashing from cover to cover, feeling their way forward, testing the enemy's resistance.

Simultaneously, the VII Reserve Corps struck the Haumont Wood (*Bois d'Haumont*), the XVIII Army Corps attacked the Caures Wood, and the III Army Corps moved against the Herbebois Wood (*Bois de l'Herbebois*). By nightfall, the Germans had taken the Haumont Wood, but not the village. French defenders clung precariously to the Herbebois Wood and the Caures Wood.

In the Caures Wood, Lieutenant Colonel Émile Driant's 56th and 59th *Chasseurs à Pied* (hunters on foot) light infantry battalions started the day with 1,300 officers and men. When the shelling stopped, about 300 survivors of the two battalions emerged from their shelters—red-eyed, blackened, deafened, and wounded—to defend the wood.

Elements of the 42nd Brigade of the German 21st Division entered the splintered wood at dusk, spearheaded by flamethrower teams and five pioneer (engineer) detachments. They came not to assault but to occupy, anticipating that no one could have lived through the day's bombardment. They were wrong. Driant's *Chasseurs* met them, and the fighting raged back and forth throughout the night.

French soldiers climb from trenches to attack the German forces.

Two battalions of French Chasseurs led by Lieutenant Colonel Émile Driant held the wood at Caures for two days, but were forced back to nearby towns. Driant was killed and only 118 Chasseurs managed to escape.

The next day, February 22, all that was left of Driant's command were seven wounded lieutenants and about a hundred *Chasseurs*. After a second day-long artillery barrage, a stronger wave of German infantry drove them back to Samogneux, Beaumont, and Ornes. Driant was killed before he could evacuate.

On February 23, similar German advances pressed steadily ahead on either side of the Caures Wood. The French outer trench lines crumbled under the incessant German pummeling, and the defenders began to withdraw. A French counterattack on the Caures Wood failed, and Brabant and Herbebois Wood fell to the Germans.

A surviving lieutenant of the French 72nd Reserve Division sent the following message to his headquarters: "The commanding officer and all company

commanders have been killed. My battalion is reduced to approximately 180 men (from 600). I have neither ammunition nor food. What am I to do?"[3]

His commander replied, "Stay in position. It is indispensable."[4] By the third day, the Germans had captured 10,000 French prisoners, 65 cannon, and 75 machine guns.

On February 24, the Brandenburg Regiment of General Ewald von Lochow's III Army Corps seized the vaunted—but virtually undefended—Fort Douaument. Church bells rang out in joyous celebration across Germany at the news. German children were given the day off from school. And Crown Prince Wilhelm showered the Brandenburg Regiment with medals. French forces teetered on the brink of defeat. However, Crown Prince Wilhelm did not press his advantage.

On February 25, a turning point in the French defense of Verdun took shape. General Noël de Castelnau, commander-in-chief General Joseph Joffre's deputy,

Wreckage of war: the remains of a French long-gun battery overrun and put out of action by a German infantry division at Verdun.

General Noël de Castelnau was a highly respected fighting general who inspired his commands in difficult time. Three of his sons gave their lives for France in World War I.

conducted an inspection tour of the Verdun sector. He found General Herr "depressed' and "a little tired."[5]

While surveying the Right (east) Bank, Castelnau made several suggestions to improve defenses. It has been said, "[W]herever he went, decision and order followed him."[6] After his inspection tour, Castelnau dispatched an order to replace the battle-weary General Herr with General Henri Philippe Pétain at Verdun.

Pétain, then commander of the French Second Army, left for Verdun right away. He telephoned ahead to XX Corps commander General Balfourier, identified himself, and issued his first order: "I have taken over command. Tell your troops. Hold fast. I have confidence in you."[7]

Balfourier replied, "That's good! Now everything is going to be all right."[8]

Jean de Pierrefeu, chronicler of the French general headquarters, described Henri Philippe Pétain this way: "I had the impression of a marble statue, of a Roman senator in a museum. Big, vigorous, of imposing figure, impassive face and pale complexion, with a direct and thoughtful glance."[9] Pétain was born to a peasant family at Cauchy-à-la-Tour in the Pas-de-Calais in 1856. He was a bachelor of sixty when he took command of the Fortified Region of Verdun.

Pétain graduated from the École Spéciale Militaire de Saint-Cyr, France's equivalent of West Point, and was commissioned in the newly formed *Chasseurs de Alpins* (Alpine Hunters) in 1876. For most of his life, Pétain disliked show and publicity. He exhibited a chronic disdain for all forms of intrigue, particularly for politics and politicians. Never shy to speak his mind, his forthright tendencies contributed to Pétain's record of slow promotions.

In 1900, Pétain reached the rank of major and assumed command of a battalion. After the start of World War I, he distinguished himself as a colonel in command of the 33rd Regiment. Promoted to general, he took command in quick succession of a brigade, a division, a corps, an army, and ultimately the Army Group Center at Bar-le-Duc.

Pétain's defensive philosophy at Verdun was *"Ils ne passeront pas!* (They shall not pass!)," which made him famous. His constant regard for the welfare of his men earned him their enthusiastic devotion. He became idolized as a national hero of France for his unyielding defense of Verdun. Pétain's later collaboration with the Nazis during World War II tarnished his otherwise splendid record as a true patriot.

General Henri Philippe Pétain

CHAPTER

FOUR

SHIFTING STRATEGIES

Pétain arrived at Verdun at 11:00 pm on February 25 and relieved Herr, whose mental state was collapsing. The new commander quickly set up his headquarters in the town hall at Souilly. He sat with his chief of staff until the early morning hours, pouring over maps and reestablishing Verdun's forts as the main defense line. (With the exception of Fort Douaumont, all of Verdun's forts remained in French hands.) Pétain then issued orders that were to be delivered to all commanders by sunup. "The right man had at last come to his greatest scene," commented military historian S. L. A. Marshall. "Verdun's defense from that hour forward was dramatically reenergized."[1]

Pétain's arrival coincided with a temporary pause in the fighting. After five days of intensive fighting, both sides were exhausted. The Germans had gained up to 3.7 miles (6 kilometers) of territory. Their heavy guns had to be brought forward to support further infantry attacks. Moving the huge mortars and artillery pieces across swampy terrain pock-marked with shell craters, in snow, rain, and cold proved difficult. Some 7,000 horses were killed in a single day.

★ ★ ★ ★ ★ ★ ★ ★ ★ ★ ★ ★ ★ ★ ★ ★ ★ ★

German guns like the Krupp 420 mm railroad howitzer, "Big Bertha," cut into the French forces. This gun was transported by five train cars and weighed 75 tons.

The decomposing body of a German soldier is a lone representative of the heavy casualties inflicted on the Germans by flanking fire by French artillery on the Left (west) Bank.

Flanking fire by French artillery on the Left (west) Bank took a heavy toll on Crown Prince Wilhelm's infantry. By the end of February, the Germans had sustained 25,000 casualties, and their offensive stagnated.

Pétain used the pause in the German attack to great advantage. He recognized that a favorable outcome to any battle depended on good logistics. German artillery had cut the single railway line to the north. Pétain designated the narrow road that led to Bar-le-Duc 50 miles (80 kilometers) away as a supply route for trucks alone. Claiming cars, vans, and trucks from all across France, he introduced the concept of supplying a modern army by motor transport. Between February 28 and March 7, 27,000 tons of supplies and 190,000 reinforcements were moved up to the front along the road that became known as the *Voie Sacrée* (Sacred Way).

Falkenhayn's original strategy had called for a limited offensive waged as a battle of attrition by artillery, not one of acquiring territory. He wanted to sit in place and blast the French into oblivion. But the Crown Prince had ideas of a grand victory, which meant forcing the French from their vaunted defenses at Verdun. Thus far, the German casualty figures nearly equaled those of the French. A change of strategy was clearly needed.

Falkenhayn and the Crown Prince and their staff met on the last day of February to rethink their plans. Initially, Falkenhayn had wanted to confine offensive actions to the Right Bank. In practice, however, flanking fire from the Left Bank and from Fort Vaux on the Right Bank was decimating the German infantry. Until those twin menaces were eliminated, German casualties would continue to mount at an unacceptable rate.

Falkenhayn reluctantly agreed to extend the offensive to the Left Bank on March 6, and to launch a second attack the next day to capture Fort Vaux on the Right Bank. The so-called Battle of the Wings was set to begin. Falkenhayn's limited offensive had already doubled in size and was growing like a wildfire in the wind.

French soldiers inside Fort Vaux prepare food rations while enjoying a brief respite from the savage fighting.

The two banks of the Meuse are distinctly different in geography: the Right Bank is ridden with gullies and steep, wooded ridges, ideal for infiltrating; the Left Bank is open, rolling country with broad, grassy slopes and wide valleys. Little cover is available, and hills provide extensive views of the surroundings. Le Mort Homme is one such hill. From its heights, the Germans could look down on Verdun itself. Along with Côte 304, Mort Homme also sheltered French artillery behind it. Accordingly, it became the main German objective—and the center of bloody, back-and-forth fighting for most of the next three months.

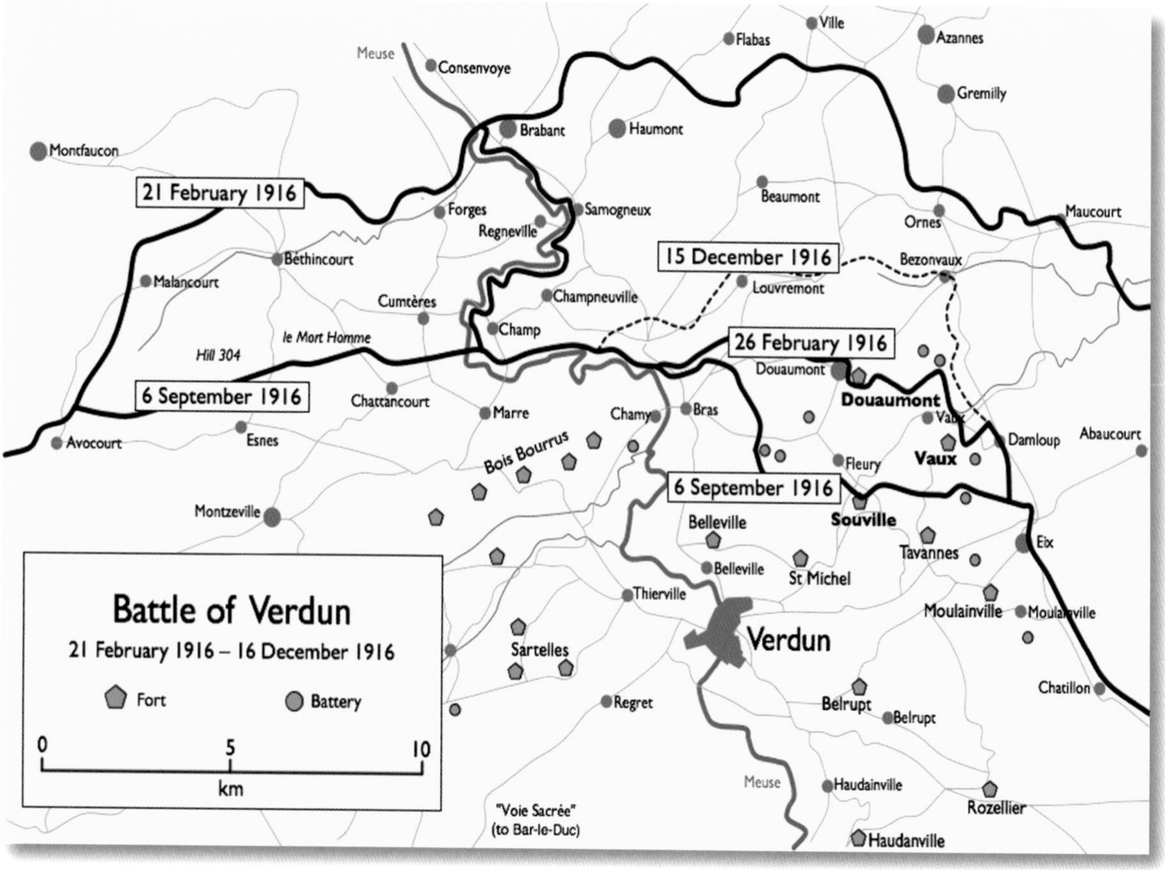

A two-dimensional view of the shifting battle lines, fort locations, battery placements, and the River Meuse running through them seems to belie the three-dimensional chaos of the live action that took place.

The triumphant figure of Death rises above a base bearing the legend *Ils ne passeront pas!* (They shall not pass!) at the memorial atop Le Mort Homme.

On March 16, the German artillery pounded Mort Homme for six hours, pouring about 120 rounds into it every minute. Eleven of the 92nd Regiment's twelve machine guns were knocked out. "Finally, the enemy judged the bombardment sufficient and launched his infantry," recalled stretcher-bearer Jean Vichy. "We fought back with bayonets. Not a foot of ground was lost."[2]

By the start of April, the Germans decided to scrap Falkenhayn's strategy of limited offensive and attack across the entire front, now twenty miles wide. Crown Prince Wilhelm launched a full-scale attack on both banks starting on April 9. The French matched every German attack with a counterattack of their own. Pétain sensed that the Germans were wearing down and issued an order of encouragement to his command. *"Courage, on les aura!* (Courage, we'll have them!)"[3] Wilhelm's last big offensive failed. Drenching rain stalled combat operations until May. By then, French casualties numbered 89,000 to 81,607 German losses.

Meanwhile, in Chantilly, General Joffre began to tire of Pétain's conduct in battle. Rotating French divisions in and out of Verdun at Pétain's call was draining resources Joffre needed for a major Allied offensive at the Somme in the summer. Rather than fire Pétain, he promoted him.

On April 19, Pétain relieved General Fernand de Langle de Cary as commander of Army Group Center, and General Robert Nivelle replaced Pétain at Verdun. In theory, Pétain would retain indirect control of the battle, but from a distance at Bar-le-Duc. In reality, front-line control shifted to Nivelle (who is credited alongside Pétain for originating France's stirring battle credo *"Ils ne passeront pas!* (They shall not pass!)"

After the failure of Wilhelm's April offensive, the Germans, in S. L. A. Marshall's words, "relapsed into nibbling tactics, taking Hill 304 at the beginning of May, Le Mort Homme at the end of the month, and Fort Vaux on June 2."[4]

General Robert Nivelle

Military strategists included aerial operations in their battle planning for the first time at Verdun. The initial German bombardment owed much of its accuracy to aerial observation. Both sides relied on intelligence collected by aerial photography during the campaign. And both sides fielded the first operational fighter squadrons at Verdun.

At the start of 1916, Germany enjoyed the advantage in the air. Its Fokker Eindecker monoplane was the first fighter equipped with a synchronized machine gun that fired through the propeller. The tide began to shift to the French Air Service in mid-February 1916.

Hordes of French bombers took to the air and relentlessly pounded German ground forces with bombs of all sizes, shapes, and description. Then a new French biplane appeared on the scene. The Nieuport 10 did not have a synchronized gun. Instead, it used a Lewis gun mounted on the upper wing. It fired by a button on the control stick. The Nieuport soon took the measure of the Eindecker, ending German aerial domination.

Two great German aces fought in the air over Verdun—Oswald Boelcke and Max Immelmann. Both aces were aerial innovators and developed tactics used by later pilots of both sides. At Boelcke's suggestion, German fighters were concentrated into squadrons called *Jagdstaffeln* (fighter squadrons).

French aces who fought at Verdun included Jean Navarre, France's "sentinel of the air," and Charles Nungesser, who scored most of his twenty-one victories there. Americans flying for France fought at Verdun in the famous *Escadrille Lafayette*.

The Nieuport 10

CHAPTER

FIVE

ENDINGS

After the fall of Fort Vaux, the Germans stood in position to assault the last ridges on the Right Bank before Verdun: Froideterre, Thiaumont, and Souville. They assigned 19 regiments to the attack. Twelve were positioned along the 3.7-mile-long (6-kilometer-long) front line. The rest were held in reserve to press whatever advantage a successful assault might bring. French General Charles Mangin described the subsequent assault as "the most important and most massive attack"[1] against Verdun.

From Souville, "it was downhill all the way to Verdun, less than two and a half miles away" noted Alistair Horne, "and once the fort fell into enemy hands it would be a matter of time before the city itself was rendered untenable."[2] General Konstantin Schmidt von Knobelsdorf, Crown Prince Wilhelm's chief of staff, optimistically boasted he would be in Verdun within three days.

On June 22, 1916, German artillery fired over 116,000 shells of diphosgene gas (Green Gas) at French artillery positions. After hearing a multitude of whistling sounds overhead, a French sergeant burst into the command post of the 130th Division and exclaimed,

Not all soldiers were lucky enough to be protected from the poison gas attacks. Some served and fought, unprotected from the ravages of poison-gas.

"Mon Général, there are shells—thousands of shells—passing overhead, that don't burst!"[3]

The general and a staff officer went outside to investigate. They heard the rumble of German guns but no explosions. Soon, as they stood listening, out of a nearby ravine crept "a pungent, sickening odor of putrefaction compounded with the mustiness of stale vinegar."[4] The horrid gas claimed over 1,600 casualties and shut down much of the French artillery. At 5:00 AM, the gas shelling stopped, and the German infantry attacked.

The next day, June 23, marked both the high point and crisis of the German offensive at Verdun. Knobelsdorf's attackers drove a 1.9-by-1.2-mile (3-by-2-kilometer) salient into the French defenses and pressed to within 3.1 miles (5 kilometers) of Verdun. They captured French strong points at Thiaumont and Froideterre and overran the village of Fleury and Chapelle Sainte-Fine. There they

German artillery blasted by the shells of the French.

stopped, exhausted, and out of water and gas shells. Knobelsdorf called off the offensive.

By the end of June, over 200,000 men had been killed or wounded on each side. The battlefield had become a place of death, destruction, and unimaginable horrors in a battle seemingly without end or prospect of victory.

Even Kaiser Wilhelm II began to doubt whether the war could be won by a single, decisive stroke. In a protest to his father, Crown Prince Wilhelm objected to continuing the carnage: "I perceived clearly that it would not be feasible to break through the stubborn defense, and that our own losses would ultimately be quite out of proportion to the gains."[5]

On July 11, the Germans mounted one final attempt to break through to Verdun, but were turned back at Fort Souville. Thereafter, they abandoned their efforts to destroy the French Army at Verdun and settled into a defensive mode. At the start of July, the main action shifted to the north of Verdun, as Allies launched a major offensive at the Somme. A relative calm fell over the Verdun sector for much of the summer.

A German soldier serving with the 65th Infantry Division in July 1916 summed up the human cost of battle in unvarnished terms:

> Anyone who has not seen these fields of carnage will never be able to imagine it. When one arrives here the shells are raining down everywhere with each step one takes but in spite of this it is necessary for everyone to go forward. One has to go out of one's way to not pass over a corpse lying at the bottom of the communication trench. Farther on, there are many wounded to tend, others who are carried back on stretchers to the rear. Some are screaming, others are pleading. One sees some who don't have legs, others without any heads, who have been left for several weeks on the ground.[6]

By the end of August, despite the sacrifices and best efforts of each German soldier, it became clear that Falkenhayn's campaign to "bleed France white" had failed. Falkenhayn resigned on August 28. General Paul von Hindenburg replaced him. After the war, Falkenhayn continued to insist that German losses at Verdun

had been "not much more than a third of those of the enemy."[7] He suffered nightmares until his death in 1922.

In October, the French opened an offensive to regain their lost territory on the Right Bank. They recaptured Fort Douaumont on October 24 and retook Fort Vaux on November 2. A final French attack on December 15 forced the Germans back over 3.1 miles (5 kilometers) from Souville. The fighting at Verdun ended on December 18.

After ten months of fighting, official French figures listed 377,231 casualties, of which 162,308 were either dead or missing. Official German figures listed 337,000 casualties, of which 100,000 were either dead or missing. The battle's combined casualty figures totaled over 700,000, of which 262,308 were either dead or missing.

About three-quarters of the French Army passed though Verdun. France lost two generations of males in the horrid battle. But their courage and resilience there restored the pride of the French Army, and bolstered the resolve of the French people to win the war. Pétain's emphasis on stubborn defense influenced French military strategists for the next two decades. Defensive thinking led to the construction of the fortified Maginot Line on France's eastern frontier. It was circumvented by the Nazi Blitzkrieg in 1940.

In December 1918, Pétain was promoted to marshal and led the victory parade down the Champs Elysée the following year. After World War II, he was tried and convicted as a war criminal for collaborating with the Nazis. Pétain was sentenced

to death, but his punishment was later reduced to life imprisonment. He died at Île d'Yeu, France, in 1951. Several attempts have been made to rebury his remains at Verdun.

Graves at Verdun

"Almost unique among the World War I battlefields where the ghosts refuse to die is Verdun,"[8] writes Alistair Horne. *Le Mort Homme,* scene of some of the fiercest fighting, "remains one of the eeriest places in Europe; the wind whistles, and no birds sing; few human beings care to enter its deserted glades."[9]

On May 8, 1916, German soldiers unwittingly brewed a pot of coffee on a box containing hand grenades and triggered an accidental explosion at Fort Douaumont. The initial blast touched off the entire ammunition magazine, killing 679 German soldiers. Unable to bring out their dead under fire by the French, the Germans blocked off a large section of the fort.

After all these years, notes C. J. Linton, "the section to this day is still blocked off and is seen as a shrine to the German dead of Verdun. Of course it is also a very haunted place, shadows in the darkness, grunts and crying have been seen and heard in this part of Douaumont."[10]

"It will be many years, if ever, before the regiments of phantoms finally march away from the hills above Verdun," remarks Colonel Leon Rodier, overseer of the Verdun battlefield sites. The ghosts refuse to go quietly. "It will be many decades before the earth gives up the last of the shells and bones that lie here."[11]

France cannot forget the dead of Verdun. "Some outsiders . . . think that, even now," writes Alistair Horne, "she is haunted by the ghosts of Verdun."[12]

The memory of soldiers like this German combatant still echoes across the Verdun countryside.

1856 Henri Philippe Pétain is born at Cauchy-à-la-Tour in the Pas-de-Calais on April 24.

1861 Erich von Falkenhayn is born at Burg Bechau, West Prussia, on November 11.

1882 Crown Prince Wilhelm is born at Potsdam, Germany, on May 6.

1914 *June 28*   Bosnian nationalist Gavrilo Princip assassinates Archduke Franz Ferdinand.

July 28   Austria-Hungary declares war on Serbia.

August 1   Germany declares war on Russia.

August 3   Germany declares war on France.

August 4   Great Britain declares war on Germany.

August 6   Austria-Hungary declares war against Russia.

1916 *February 21*   Battle of Verdun begins.

February 22   Caures Wood falls to Germans; Lieutenant Colonel Driant is killed.

February 23   Brabant and Herbebois Wood fall to the Germans.

February 24   The Brandenburg Regiment seizes Fort Douaument.

February 25   General Henri Philippe Pétain takes command at Verdun.

March 6   The VI German Reserve Army Corps advances on Le Mort Homme.

March 16   German artillery pounds Le Mort Homme.

April 9   Germans attack along entire Verdun front.

May 8   German soldiers accidentally trigger explosion at Fort Douaumont, killing 679.

June 2   Fort Vaux falls to the Germans.

July 11   Germans mount final attempt to break through to Verdun.

August 28   Falkenhayn resigns.

October 24   French recapture Fort Douaumont.

November 2   French retake Fort Vaux.

December 15   Final French attack forces Germans back more than 3.1 miles (5 kilometers) from Souville.

December 18   Battle of Verdun ends.

1918 Pétain is promoted to marshal.

1919 He leads a victory parade down the Champs Elysées.

1922 General Erich von Falkenhayn dies at Lindstadt, Germany, on April 8.

1951 Crown Prince Wilhelm dies in Hechingen, Germany, on July 20; Pétain dies at Île d'Yeu, France, on July 23.

Chapter 1 The Longest Battle
1. John Keegan, *The First World War* (New York: Alfred A. Knopf, 1999), p. 283.
2. Battle of Verdun: Phase 3, http://wereldoorlog1418.nl/battleverdun/battleverdun33/index.htm
3. Ibid.
4. Paranormal History, www.freewebs.com/paranormalhistory/apps/blog/show/1686662-verdun-bienvenue-l-enfer

Chapter 2 Prelude to Battle
1. John Keegan, *The First World War* (New York: Alfred A. Knopf, 1999), p. 278.
2. Ibid.
3. Ibid., p. 279.
4. S. L. A. Marshall, *World War I* (New York: American Heritage, 1985), p. 244.
5. Alistair Horne, *The Price of Glory: Verdun 1916* (New York: Penguin Books, 1993), p. 68.
6. Marshall, p. 235.
7. Horne, p. 352.
8. Chris McNab, *Verdun 1916.* Battle Story Series. (Stroud, UK: The History Press, 2013), p. 37.

Chapter 3 Turning Point
1. S. L. A. Marshall, *World War I* (New York: American Heritage, 1985), p. 244.
2. Battle of Verdun: Phase 2, http://wereldoorlog1418.nl/battleverdun/battleverdun22/index.htm
3. John Keegan, *The First World War* (New York: Alfred A. Knopf, 1999), p. 281.
4. William Martin, *Verdun 1916: "They Shall Not Pass."* Campaign Series. (Oxford, UK: Osprey Publishing, 2001), p. 40.
5. Alistair Horne, *The Price of Glory: Verdun 1916* (New York: Penguin Books, 1993), p. 129.
6. Ibid.
7. Ibid., p. 143.
8. Ibid., p. 144.
9. Ibid., p. 133.

Chapter 4 Shifting Strategies
1. S. L. A. Marshall, *World War I* (New York: American Heritage, 1985), p. 247.
2. William Martin, *Verdun 1916: "They Shall Not Pass."* Campaign Series (Oxford, UK: Osprey Publishing, 2001), p. 48.
3. Ibid., p. 49.
4. Marshall, p. 248.

Chapter 5 Endings
1. Spencer C. Tucker, "Verdun" in *The European Powers in the First World War: An Encyclopedia.* Edited by Spencer C. Tucker (New York: Garland Publishing,1999), p. 717.
2. Alistair Horne, *The Price of Glory: Verdun 1916* (New York: Penguin Books, 1993), p. 284.
3. Ibid., p. 285.
4. Ibid., p. 286.
5. William Martin, *Verdun 1916: "They Shall Not Pass."* Campaign Series (Oxford, UK: Osprey Publishing, 2001), p. 72.
6. Chris McNab, *Verdun 1916. Battle Story Series.* (Stroud, UK: The History Press, 2013), p. 101.
7. Alistair Horne, *The Price of Glory: Verdun 1916* (New York: Penguin Books, 1993), p. 335.
8. Alistair Horne, "The Longest Battle," www.nytimes.com/1991/02/17/travel/the-longest battle,html?pagewanted=print&src=pm
9. Ibid.
10. Paranormal History, www.freewebs.com/paranormalhistory/apps/blog/show/1686662-verdun-bienvenue-l-enfer
11. Patrick Bishop, "Life returns to Verdun killing fields 85 years on," *The Telegraph,* www.telegraph.co.uk/news/worldnews/europe/france/1339966/Life-returns-to-Verdun-killing-fields-85-years-on.html
12. Alistair Horne, "The Longest Battle," *The New York Times,* www.nytimes.com/1991/02/17/travel/the-longest battle,html?pagewanted=print&src=pm

Books

Barber, Nicola. *World War I*. North Mankato, MN: Heinemann, 2012.

Conway, John. *World War I: A MyReportLinks.com Book*. U. S. Wars Series. Berkeley Heights, NJ: Enslow Publishers, 2003.

Green, Robert. *World War I*. World History Series. Farmington Hills, MI: Lucent Books, 2007.

Hunter, Nick. *Campaigns of World War I*. Remembering World War I Series.

North Mankato, MN: Heinemann, 2014.

Kent, Zachary. *World War I: From the Lusitania to Versailles*. The United States at War Series. Berkeley Heights, NJ: Enslow Publishers, 2011.

Works Consulted

Corvisier, André, ed. *A Dictionary of Military History*. English edition edited, revised, and expanded by John Childs. Translated by Chris Turner. Oxford, UK:

Blackwell Publishers, 1994.

Cowley, Robert, and Geoffrey Parker, eds. *The Reader's Companion to Military History*. New York: Houghton Mifflin Company, 1996.

Davies, Norman. *Europe: A History*. New York: Oxford University Press, 1996.

Davis, Paul K. *100 Decisive Battles from Ancient Times to the Present*. New York: Oxford University Press, 2001.

DuPuy, R. Ernest, and Trevor N. Dupuy. *The Encyclopedia of Military History from 3500 B. C. to the Present*. Rev. ed. New York: Harper & Row, 1977.

Eggenberger, David. *An Encyclopedia of Battles: Accounts of Over 1,560 Battles from 1479 B. C. to the Present*. New York: Dover Publications, 1985.

Ellis, John. *Eye-Deep in Hell: Trench Warfare in World War I.* New York: Pantheon Books, 1976.

Ferguson, Niall. *The Pity of War.* New York: Basic Books, 1999.

Haythornwaite, Philip J. *The World War I Sourcebook.* London: Arms and Armour Press, 1994.

Holmes, Richard, ed. *The Oxford Companion to Military History.* New York: Oxford University Press, 2001.

Horne, Alistair. *The Price of Glory: Verdun 1916.* New York: Penguin Books, 1993.

Jablonski, Edward. *A Pictorial History of the World War I Years.* Garden City, NY: Doubleday and Company, 1979.

Keegan, John. *The Face of Battle.* New York: Penguin Books, 1985.

———. *The First World War.* New York: Alfred A. Knopf, 1999.

Marshall, S. L. A. *World War I.* New York: American Heritage, 1985.

Martin, William. *Verdun 1916: "They Shall Not Pass." Campaign Series.* Oxford, UK: Osprey Publishing, 2001.

McNab, Chris. *Verdun 1916. Battle Story Series.* Stroud, UK: The History Press, 2013.

Messenger, Charles. *The Century of Warfare: Worldwide Conflict from 1900 to the Present Day.* New York: HarperCollins, 1995.

Strachan, Hew. *The Oxford Illustrated History of World War I.* New York: Oxford University Press, 1998.

Taylor, A. J. P. *The First World War and its Aftermath.* London: The Folio Society, 1998.

Tucker, Spencer C. *The European Powers in the First World War: An Encyclopedia.* New York: Garland Publishing, 1999.

Young, Peter, and Michael Calvert. *A Dictionary of Battles 1816–1976.* New York: Mayflower Books, 1978.

On the Internet

Battle of Verdun: Phase 2

http://wereldoorlog1418.nl/battleverdun/battleverdun22/index.htm

Battle of Verdun: Phase 3

http://wereldoorlog1418.nl/battleverdun/battleverdun33/index.htm

The New York Times

www.nytimes.com/1991/02/17/travel/the-longest-battle,html?pagewanted=print&src=pm

Osprey Publishing: The Destination for Military History
http:/www.ospreypublishing.com/articles/world_war_1/fire_kills_marshal_

petain_and_the_ghosts_of_verdun/

Paranormal History: Verdun

www.freewebs.com/paranormalhistory/apps/blog/show/1686662-verdun-bienvenue-l-enfer

The Telegraph

www.telegraph.co.uk/news/worldnews/europe/france/1339966/Life-returns-to- Verdun-killing-fields-85-years-on.html

GLOSSARY

attrition (uh-TRIH-shun)—A gradual wearing down of strength and morale by continuous harassment, abuse, or attack.

chasseur (sha-SUHR)—One of a body of light cavalry or infantry trained for rapid maneuvering.

diphosgene (dy-FOZ-jeen)—A liquid compound $C_2Cl_4O_2$ used as a poison gas in World War I.

entente (ahn-TAHNT)—An international understanding providing for a common course of action; a coalition of parties to an entente.

marshal (MAHR-shul)—A general officer of the highest military rank.

pioneer (py-uh-NEER)—A member of a military unit usually of construction engineers.

putrefaction (pyew-truh-FAK-shun)—The decomposition of organic matter.

redoubt (rih-DOWT)—A small, temporary, enclosed defensive work; a defended position; stronghold.

requisition (reh-kwuh-ZI-shun)—The act of formally requiring or calling upon someone to perform a task.

salient (SAYL-yint)—A projecting part of a fort, trench, or line of defense.

strategy (STRAH-tuh-jee)—The planning and directing of the whole operation of a campaign or war.

tactic (TAK-tik)—The art of placing or maneuvering forces skillfully in a battle.

INDEX